THINKING
ABOUT E

100 Perspectives (

Here are samples of the social media feedback
given over the first 100 days.
(from Facebook, Instagram and LinkedIn)

Brilliant! / Inspirational! / Love it! / Wise words... / Put
these musings into a book please! / Good one, Des! /
Beautiful. / These are really good! / Loving this series,
thanks! / Yet another thought-provoking masterpiece.
/ Such a beautiful thought! / The exercises help me so
much, thanks / Super series! / Thank you, Des for the daily
inspiration. / Such immense truth. / Really like these. /
Ooh, loving these. / I needed this today, thank-you. / So
thought provoking. / These get better every day! / What a
powerful thought! / WOW! / These are wonderful posts,
love them so much. / Yes Des, nailed it again! / Wonderful
words. / Such immense truth in these! / Simply perfect! /
Love these! / Exceptional questions and inspiring thoughts.
/ Please put these into a book. / Amazing posts! / These are
so cool! / Going to share these! / So beautiful / This is my
favourite—so far! / Incredibly thought provoking. / Love all
of these — so creative! / These posts are so inspiring.

[Handwritten inscription:] Dear Thanks for hosting a mega session! See you soon De

THINKING
DIFFERENTLY
ABOUT
EVERYTHING

100 Perspectives on What Really Matters

DES MCCABE

NEW ACTIVITY PUBLICATIONS

NEW ACTIVITY
PUBLICATIONS

Published by New Activity Publications
(a not for profit publisher)

ISBN – 978-1-904969-58-7

www.workitout.info/desblog

For the amazing McCabe clan
in Northern Ireland, England and the U.S.A.,
with love.

Contents

Des McCabe's Daily Blog

When the lockdown due to the Covid-19 virus started, it struck me how everything had changed overnight. I began to reflect on many of the things we can take for granted in work, business and life – so I started a daily blog called 'Thinking Differently About Everything'

I set myself the task of taking a common business or work phrase every day and to 're-think' it. In other words, I wanted to bring my own experience and knowledge to that word and what it means to me. You of course, will have your own reflections and perspectives on each word also, so please capture and write down your thoughts as you go through the book.

A Personal Development Process

This is a different kind of work and business book. It uses common words in business and life that we know and encourages us to reflect on them from a personal perspective.

This collection of perspectives was never intended to be a book of poetry or prose. First and foremost, it was created as a personal training process. The purpose is simply to encourage and help you think about your future, your career and your priorities to acquire greater clarity on all that really matters to you.

This is why after each of the perspectives you will find a short Personal Development Exercise with one of two questions to help you look at things a bit differently.

We know that irrespective of what has happened in the past that we cannot go backwards. We will not go back to where we were before the virus. The challenge therefore, for each of us, is to think differently about everything and reflect on what really matters to us so that we can create new options, opportunities and pathways together.

Use a Journal and Capture Everything

As you work through these perspectives and the Personal Development Exercises, you will notice that your thinking will become more 'open'. You will have some thoughts arising directly from the activity, but you will also carry this approach into the rest of your day leading to greater creativity and focus in all aspects of your life and work.

Think about the Personal Development Exercise questions. Record your thoughts and ideas. Regularly review all of your notes. What are the key messages coming through? What pointers or actions does this suggest for moving forward?

Try and use a journal right from the outset to capture your ideas and thoughts. Write something in this every single day (or every time you read one of the perspectives). It doesn't matter if you write just one sentence, a random thought or a question. It is the writing process that captures and embeds the personal learning and will give you the greatest benefits.

Your journal will become the 'idea hub', a 'source file' and a 'launchpad' for the next stage of your journey.

Perspectives Are Starting Points

Enjoy my perspectives but remember that this is a book where my content isn't the priority. My perspectives are there simply as starting points or examples to encourage you to create your perspectives for these words.

So, for each word, write your story and say what it means to you. Come up with your quotes. Create poems that don't rhyme. Put in jokes. Challenge yourself on the big stuff that matters. Remember those important to you. Think about your health. Write about what makes you truly happy. Reconnect to all that has gone before and all that is relevant now. Mix business, work and life in new ways. Have fun!

This personal development approach offers the chance to connect meaning and purpose with our daily routine and responsibilities. It brings all elements of our lives together as one enterprise.

Have your journal as you read each perspective and just start writing. Write whatever comes. Allow it to flow and grow.

Five Ways to Use the Perspectives

From the feedback gathered over the first 100 days, it is clear that people were using the perspectives in five main ways to expand their own thinking and development.

1. Quick read

When we read a famous quotation, we sometimes get a sense of encouragement or hope. Many people will read the perspectives initially in this way, with a similar mindset, to see if it resonates with their own views or aspirations.

2. Daily routine

A second way is to take one perspective each day (for about 10-15 minutes) and work your way through the book, reflecting on each of the perspectives, completing the Personal Development Exercise questions and adding your own thoughts and ideas. The process can become a part of your daily routine, enabling you to build upon your own personal development process.

3. Short boost

Some people decide on a shorter fixed timescale at the outset (say 7, 21 or 30 days) and allocate 15-20 minutes per day to explore some of the themes and perspectives in this book. One person chose two different perspectives to work with each day. You may find the index at the back of the book useful in choosing your perspectives.

This process can be repeated with different perspectives to create a longer development process.

4. Add your own 'Thinking Differently' perspectives

In addition to one or more of the approaches above, some people will set themselves the challenge of adding their own personal perspective for each of the daily words in this book.

To do this, ask yourself 'What does this word mean to me?' or 'If I were writing a perspective for this word, what would I say?' You can then capture and write down your thoughts in your journal.

5. Create New 'Thinking Differently' Perspectives

And finally, some people choose their own words which are not listed here and create their own fresh perspectives. Think of words you come across regularly and re-think what they mean to you personally.

Use stories, examples and memories to capture the real meaning for you. Be creative. Be kind. Be radical. Be challenging to yourself and those around you. Confront the traditional definition, question your work in this moment, evaluate today, take stock of your year and have fun!

Here are a few words to get you started but feel free to choose your own. Homework, Health and Safety, Virus, Product Launch, Customer Service Desk, Promotion, Opportunity, Retirement, Value, Happy Hour, Visiting Times, Official, Time out, Mobile, etc!

There are many variations on each of the approaches above so, feel free to change or adapt them if you think there is something that would work better for you.

'Thinking Differently About Everything' offers us the opportunity to create a world which is kinder, more compassionate and more sustainable. It's a future that supports all of us and helps each of us to fulfil our true potential. Thank you for working with me and enjoy the process!

The Perspectives

Days 1-100

Day 1

Asset Management

Imagine if your new work
coincided completely
with what you
really wanted to do.

Imagine if you could
use your gifts and skills
to achieve all that
really mattered to you.

Imagine if you could
design your future
rather than wait
to see what happens.

Imagine if you used
all that you are and
all that you have learned
in new ways.

PERSONAL DEVELOPMENT EXERCISE

- What do you really want to do?
- What are your assets – your skills, experience, knowledge and interests?
- How can you use these in different and new ways?

Day 2

Entrepreneurship

We are the entrepreneurs of life
not slaves of the past
or prisoners of expectation.

We are the entrepreneurs of life
looking after all our global neighbours
and caring for our beautiful world.

We are the entrepreneurs of life
re-thinking, creating, shaping and building
a different way, in our own way.

We are the glorious, beautiful,
gentle, kind, visionary and
successful entrepreneurs of life.

PERSONAL DEVELOPMENT EXERCISE

- Entrepreneurship relates to all aspects of our lives – not just business creation.
- Can you think of five areas, ways, situations or relationships where you can be more entrepreneurial?

Day 3

Currency Flipping

Some say that
business is about doing and
spirituality is about being.

These are the two sides
of the coin of life–doing and being.
They sit together within each of us.

But the two sides face in opposite directions
so unfortunately, cannot be viewed
at the same time.

We have to consciously choose to flip over the coin.
Then we get the full picture for a moment.
We see everything in totality.

But what if we could sit
on the edge of the coin
and touch both sides together at the same time?

Doing and being.
The edge of the coin.
Business and spirituality as one.

PERSONAL DEVELOPMENT EXERCISE

- In a sentence write down what spirituality means to you.
- The language of business and spirituality are very different. Make two lists of five words in each area that are rarely used in the other areas.
- How might business and spirituality link together to create new perspectives, questions and opportunities for all?

Day 4

Interest Rates

What is your level of interest
in the job that you do?
Do you give your best in every situation
and to every person?

Do you encourage, motivate
and inspire others?
Are you positive,
enthusiastic and helpful?

Do you always give 100%
to the work that you do?
If we can increase our interest rate,
we'll all enjoy greater returns.

PERSONAL DEVELOPMENT EXERCISE

- Where are you investing your time, energy and experience?
- What are the key relationships that you want to invest more into?
- How will you measure your returns?

Day 5

Job Specification

Your life is changing.
It will not be the same again.
You will not go back
to where you were.

You've already gone off
in a different direction
and are doing things differently.
Living in different ways.

Stop and take stock.
Capture what has been good
and cherish these things.
Do not lose what you've become.

A high price has been paid by many
for what we have been given.
We carry their dreams and go forward
as we build a different way.

PERSONAL DEVELOPMENT EXERCISE

- How has your life changed as a result of events linked to the Covid-19 virus outbreak?
- What have you to cherish?
- How will you use this learning and period of discovery to build a different way?

Day 6

Profits

We are all called as prophets when we are born.
To stand up for what is right, to go against the crowd
and to give a voice to those who have none.

We are all called to use our talents and gifts in all
moments and in all circumstances. Gifts of listening,
writing, speaking, fixing, making and organising.

We are all called to learn from our experience as we
journey, for wisdom is the fruit of age. It needs the
nourishment of continuing along the right path.

We are all called for a purpose.
Today has its purpose for us and
we must seek it with all of our being.

We are all called to be with God -not in some
religious way that is detached from the 'real' world
but, in a way that goes to the heart of our very being.

We are all called as prophets–to be truly ourselves.

PERSONAL DEVELOPMENT EXERCISE

- What does the word profit mean to you?
- What does the word prophet mean to you?
- What (if any) are the points of overlap?

Day 7

Social Influencers

In these days of enforced isolation
send out your message of kindness
on Facebook, Twitter, LinkedIn,
YouTube, Instagram or TikTok.

You can change lives
with your encouragement, stories,
experience, guidance or expertise.
And you may never know about it.

So, do not worry about likes,
shares or feedback.
Those who need your help
or advice will find you.

The approval of others is irrelevant
for this is only vanity.
Capture your thoughts, be brave
and put your love out there.

Remember, the biggest 'like' is yourself
and valuing all that you are.
The biggest 'share' is when you
offer this to everyone.

PERSONAL DEVELOPMENT EXERCISE

Fifty years ago, Joe Karbo said that each of us knows more about something than half of the people in the world.

- What is your area of experience?
- How can you help others?
- How will you share your expertise?

Day 8

Policy Review

Life is hard for many people.
We lose those we love.
We suffer personal disappointments and setbacks.
We struggle to pay for the things we need.
We worry about those close to us.

Most of this people carry to work.
Where little is said.

Kindness is the foundation of wellbeing.
It's a gentle way of being.
It's helping when you can without being asked.
It's checking quietly if all is okay.
It's time to write our Kindness Policy.

PERSONAL DEVELOPMENT EXERCISE

- Draft a Kindness Policy for your workplace, group or family.
- What is the purpose of the Policy?
- How will it work?
- What should it achieve?

Day 9

Household Management

Lightbulb Managers

Visionaries with a caring and responsive approach to others.

- They shine
- They provide inspiration for others
- They are most visible when things are tough
- They respond immediately
- They are consistent
- They do not discriminate with their support

Wardrobe Managers

Possess strong organisation, presentation and personal development skills.

- They review of objectives each morning
- They plan their weeks in advance
- They regularly add new skills and review resources
- They clear out the deadwood as required
- They are very aware of first impressions

Attic Managers

Seen as largely inaccessible and irrelevant in today's business.

- They hoard (take rather than give)
- They work in the dark
- They are locked away and are rarely seen.
- They are held with some sentimental value until the big clear out.
- They relate best to children and older people.
- They cherish only the past.

PERSONAL DEVELOPMENT EXERCISE

- What type of household manager are you?
- Can you create another house related category that reflects different attitudes, behaviours or aspects of management?

Day 10

Management Buyout

I reinvented my life today.
I created a whole new way of being.
I redefined who I am
and what I am about.
I left behind my old life,
my previous world.

I still know all the same people
but I see them through different glasses
now clearer and brighter.
Today I created a whole new way of being.
I'm a different person
in the same skin.

PERSONAL DEVELOPMENT EXERCISE

- If you were to reinvent your life today what would it look like?
- What is your new way of being?

Day 11

Wealth Creation

The contract for sharing
called the seller and buyer
is flawed because it involves
the exchange of money.

This excludes so many
that wish to benefit
from your products,
services or experience.

People may never know
the value of what you can offer
or simply may not
have the money to buy.

They may live in
other parts of the world
where the cost of your expertise
is beyond their reach.

Give away your stuff for free,
build real relationships and
create a sharing global economy
where all can participate equally.

For your real wealth lies
not in limited financial transactions
but in the spread of your gifts
outwards and onwards forever.

PERSONAL DEVELOPMENT EXERCISE

- What are the three greatest gifts (knowledge, experience or expertise) that you have been blessed with?
- How can you begin today to share just one of these with others for free?

Day 12

Hitting Targets

If you throw a stone
to hit a stick in the water,
you can easily miss.
Try again.

If you keep repeating this
you can miss many times
using up your resources
and time.

You can however pick up a handful of pebbles
and throw them all together
easily bombarding your target,
instantly.

PERSONAL DEVELOPMENT EXERCISE

- What targets are you trying to hit – at work, at home, relationships, personal, health, career, future, etc?
- Where are your pebbles?

Day 13

Breakfast Briefing

Awaken slowly and gently.
Be careful as the day stumbles clumsily
into your stories of night,
trying hard not to stand
on delicate fragments of your dreams.

Let them dance together,
your night and day,
looking strangely at each other,
finding a place with each other,
for these fleeting moments.

Hover between your conscious
and subconscious with due reverence
for glimpses of your unknown.
Let this unseen world
unfold its magic.

For the day will soon be here
and the possibilities of night
may be gone forever.
In the moment,
let them play together.

PERSONAL DEVELOPMENT EXERCISE

- What glimpses have you had of your unknown?
- How might you capture and treasure the fragments of your dreams?

Day 14

Lockdown

Peter May wrote a book
in 2005 called Lockdown.
It was rejected by publishers
for being 'extremely unrealistic
and unreasonable'.

For fifteen years his story
about a virus transforming all our lives
could not be imagined.
Then a week ago,
Lockdown was finally published.

So how do we imagine
the next fifteen years
for our lives, for our family,
for starving children, for our planet,
for society and for peace?

For Lockdown is more than a book
or a state of social isolation.
Lockdown is our freedom
to create the 'extremely unrealistic
and unreasonable'.

PERSONAL DEVELOPMENT EXERCISE

- What is the 'extremely unrealistic and unreasonable' future that you would like to see unfold?
- Write down your story, please!

Day 15

Science Based

My three-year-old granddaughter
explained to me
that the glass isn't
half full or
half empty.

It's all full.
Half full of water
and half full of air.
Sometimes we don't see
the full picture.

PERSONAL DEVELOPMENT EXERCISE

- What's in your glass?
- What are the visible and invisible parts of your life?

Day 16

Mental Health

The fog had arrived.
It stopped all traffic
in and out.

The internal systems
couldn't function,
stuck in neutral.

Life goes on.
Maintenance tasks get done,
nothing else.

All communication
had ceased.
Nothing is there.

The fog usually disperses
in a day.
This is taking longer.

Two days on
all is gridlocked.
Maybe tomorrow.

PERSONAL DEVELOPMENT EXERCISE

- What is your fog?
- What impact does it have on you?
- When and how does your fog clear?

Day 17

Photocopying

To make money just copy
someone else's product or business.
I'm sure you can make it
cheaper or improve it.

Add a new feature,
make it faster,
quicker acting
or longer lasting.

To change lives
and change the world,
create your own solution.
Are you still photocopying?

PERSONAL DEVELOPMENT EXERCISE

- How much of what you do is photocopying?
- What is your idea to make things better in our world or to help others?
- What's the first step?

Day 18

Diversifying

Networking with flowers.
Growing rainbows.
Building waves.
Talking to carrots.
Waiting on seahorses.
Holding time.
Investing in mornings.
Collecting clouds.

PERSONAL DEVELOPMENT EXERCISE

- Can you escape from your normal thinking and behaviour?
- Can you create totally out of the box concepts that bring you into a new space?

Day 19

Waiting Room

It's a strange place.
Sitting alone in this waiting room
wondering when the train will arrive.
Indeed, if it will arrive
and if it will stop here.

I am stuck here, helpless
between Good Friday and Easter Sunday
on this silent Saturday, sitting and waiting.
Between death and life.
Between this world and eternity.

PERSONAL DEVELOPMENT EXERCISE

Waiting rooms are interesting places. They hold us for a time
between where we were and where we are going.

- Where are you on your journey?
- What are you waiting on at this moment?

(This was written on Holy Saturday between Good Friday and
Easter Sunday)

Day 20

Easter Sunday

The front door will open soon
and we shall walk out
with gratitude and joy.
Off for a coffee.
To meet up with friends,
to be together and laugh again.

The front door will open soon
and we shall walk out,
with gratitude and joy.
Remembering all.
To a different life, a better way
and our new beginning.

PERSONAL DEVELOPMENT EXERCISE

- When Covid-19 has passed, what will be your gratitude and joy?
- What will have been your new beginning?

Day 21

Battery Life

Each morning without fail
the sun rises on the horizon.
Slowly emerging into full view
so bright that I cannot look for long.

Each morning without fail
the sun rises on the horizon
whatever the circumstances
whatever I'm doing.

Each morning without fail
the sun rises on the horizon.
Before I was here and after I am gone
the sun rises on the horizon.

PERSONAL DEVELOPMENT EXERCISE

- Make a plan to sit and watch a sunrise.
- Take a journal (and camera) with you.

Day 22

Free Range

We are trapped like chickens
snatching at all in front of us.
We are going nowhere fast,
doing more of the same in our cage.
Just like everyone else.

The tiny baby is asleep in her cot.
Snug as a bug in a rug.
Content and happy.
Watched over by her mother and father,
and has not a care in the world.

Let us step out of our cage
with the mindset of a child
to just be our selves.
To trust in love
and sleep in peace.

PERSONAL DEVELOPMENT EXERCISE

- What is a free range human?
- What will be different for us when we escape from our lockdown?

Day 23

Leap Year

The core personal development question is
'what am I really capable of?'
The response isn't
about business, work or money.

It's about who we are and
looking beyond our perceived limitations.
It's about growing into our capacity
even if we cannot perceive it fully.

This is the search for something
we never thought we would look at
even though deep down
we know we have the potential.

This is the leapfrog.
It's not linear, cumulative or predictable.
It's about us leaving our lily pad
and just going.

PERSONAL DEVELOPMENT EXERCISE

- What are you really capable of?
- What have you never thought you could do?
- What does your new lily pad look like?

Day 24

SWOT Analysis

'The Hide Away Pub'.
Can you turn
your greatest perceived weakness
into your biggest asset?

PERSONAL DEVELOPMENT EXERCISE

- SWOT means Strengths, Weaknesses, Opportunities and Threats.
- What is you greatest perceived limitation (weakness) at the moment?
- List five possible ways to get over, around or through this.

Day 25

Operating System

Spirituality is not something airy-fairy.
It is simply the way that we give meaning
to all that we are and all that we do.
It is the fabric of who we are.

Spiritually isn't outside of us
or detached from us.
It is our operating system
silently working away.

PERSONAL DEVERLOPMENT EXERCISE

- How would you define your operating system?
- What keeps you going?
- How often do you check, service or update your operating system?

Day 26

Outside Catering

The boss and employee relationship
is deeply flawed.
It is not a true construct
for it restricts both parties.

We can only bring a fixed menu
to the job table.
Providing the same meals every day
in every workplace.

We all leave behind
kitchens full of food,
unused equipment and
recipe books unopened.

PERSONAL DEVELOPMENT EXERCISE

- List all of the skills, experience, interests and knowledge that you leave at home when you go to work.
- What new 'recipe' might you create today?
- How will you build your 'Outside Catering' business?

Day 27

Multi-faith

You do not need to have faith
to fulfil your purpose.
You do not need to have any religion
to fulfil your purpose.

Your purpose is love.
For love is our faith and our religion.
Unique in each of us, in all that we are
and all that we are here to do.

PERSONAL DEVELOPMENT EXERCISE

- Write down your personal definitions for each of the following
  three words – faith, religion and love.

Day 28

Key Worker

Are you looking for more clients,
slowly building your email list
or trying to learn online marketing?

Are you promoting yourself or your business?
Do you use Facebook or Instagram and do all the 'stuff'
you hear so much about on the internet?

Are you being sucked into apps or
websites that promise amazing opportunities
but cost you money?

Have you been on training courses
or webinars that always
end up selling to you?

You can spend a fortune on other peoples' products
trying to earn more money
and build your future.

You can waste your precious time
chasing activities and learning the latest things
that just don't count.

Do what you should be doing.
Follow your own path
and use your skills to help others.

PERSONAL DEVELOPMENT EXERCISE

- How would you describe your path?
- How can you use your skills and experience in more ways and in new ways to help others?

Day 29

Stocktake

My *display until* date is Thursday.
My *best before* date is Friday.
My *use by* date is Saturday.
My recycling date is Sunday.

When should I take stock?

PERSONAL DEVELOPMENT EXERCISE

- What are you including in your next personal stocktake?
- What are you measuring and counting?
- How often do you need to stocktake?

Day 30

Inclusion

Inclusion is made real
through the rain
watering all of our crops
wherever they may be.
No preconditions,
no preferences.
Reliably and consistently.

Inclusion is made real
through the sunshine
warming all of us
wherever we may be.
No preconditions,
no preferences.
Reliably and consistently.

Inclusion is made real
through each of us
reaching out to others
wherever they may be.
No preconditions,
no preferences.
Reliably and consistently.

PERSONAL DEVELOPMENT EXERCISE

- Does your inclusion policy at work focus on everyone or only certain categories of people? How might you begin to change this?
- On a personal level, who are you reaching out to?

Day 31

Needs Analysis

Sometimes there is
no need to think
no need to speak
no need to act.

Sometimes we
just need to stop
just need to sit
just need to be.

PERSONAL DEVELOPMENT EXERCISE

- Find a quiet place with no distractions. Sit down and relax. Try and empty you brain of all thoughts. Deliberately leave a space of nothingness. Keep coming back to this emptiness. Just be.
- At the finish time, write down what happened and what you've learned.
- Repeat the above process every day for five days.

Day 32

Give and Take

In the world of want I strive for more.
More income, a bigger house or a better job.
Recognition, popularity or a sense of importance.

In the world of plenty I have more than I need.
From this place I can reach out to you,
free to share all that I have and all that I am.

PERSONAL DEVELOPMENT EXERCISE

- List five situations when you have been in the world of more.
- List five situations when you have been in the world of plenty.
- What do these ten points tell you about yourself?

Day 33

Assimilation Effect

My perfect day is made up of
hundreds of imperfect moments.
Each one is amazing and magical
and yet not perfect.

You see, this day isn't just a collection
of hundreds of imperfect moments
but rather a unique composition
that makes today perfect.

It's a realisation and an understanding
that goes beyond the individual pieces
of each day and pulls together a picture
that is perfection in itself.

I go beyond a 'sum of the parts' valuation.
I look beyond the moments and activities
and realise just what is happening
with me, within me and around me.

Perfect happiness exists in each of us
in all of those imperfect, day to day interactions
and unique moments that characterise
who and what we are.

PERSONAL DEVELOPMENT EXERCISE

- Write down some of the imperfect moments of your day–taking today or yesterday as your case study. Why was each of these moments imperfect?

- Now, 'flip' each of these and ask what was the 'unique moment' in each interaction or activity for you?

- How do you look back on this day in its entirety?

Day 34

Meditation Masterclass

And when nothing happens,
nothing seems to work and
there is no conversation,
then recognise that this is
about just sitting and just being.

There is no need for productivity.
There is no need for thought.
There is no need for inspiration.
Just sit with no expectation.
Just relax. Just be in that moment.

For our failure to meditate or reflect
or pray or even sit, takes us closer
to our greatest success.
When the world wants to drag us back,
stay with the failure.

PERSONAL DEVELOPMENT EXERCISE

- Create some 'me time' and just sit on your own with no thoughts or expectations.
- Write down what happens–and remember there is no such thing as 'failure' or 'this doesn't work for me'.
- Repeat this process when you can.

Day 35

Contribution

If we are not different
we are just more of the same.

PERSONAL DEVELOPMENT EXERCISE

- We are different to others and we all have a different contribution to make. What is your contribution?

- Our future life is not just 'more of the same'. It is not just extending what has happened up to now. How will you be different?

Day 36

De-clutter

Clear out your office.
Empty your cabinets and
get rid of your old papers.
Close the door behind you.

We don't have to continue doing
what we've always done.
We don't have to carry
all of our imperfect pasts with us.

We can dispose of our papers and
separate out what we no longer need.
We can start afresh
from wherever we are.

Unburden yourself from your past.
Leave boxes and bags behind.
Take only that which gives you
joy, peace and happiness.

PERSONAL DEVELOPMENT EXERCISE

- Are you ready to clear out 'your office'? What do you no longer need to hold onto?
- What is it that gives you joy, peace and happiness?
- What does your 'fresh start' look like?

-

Day 37

Ambition

The main task that you're working on
at the moment is really a small thing.
Beyond this there is a larger task
that you are easily capable of.
Just think for a moment
what is this larger task?
For this is what you should be doing.
This should be your focus.

And beyond this larger task
is a greater task one of real significance,
that you are easily capable of.
Just think for a moment
what is this greater task?
For this is what you should be doing.
This should be your focus.

And beyond this greater task
is the greatest task
where all of your effort should be,
that you are easily capable of.
Just think for a moment
what is the greatest task?
For this is what you should be doing.
This should be your focus.

PERSONAL DEVELOPMENT EXERCISE

- What is the key task that you are working on now?
- What is the 'larger task', the 'greater task' beyond this and the 'greatest task'?
- What is the level of your ambition?

Day 38

Click and Collect

Sometimes we can act like a tortoise
moving very slowly,
step-by-step,
sometimes making progress,
and sometimes
standing still.

But what if we were a seagull
kicking off from a standing start?
Zooming at great pace,
covering vast distances,
deciding where to land and
immediately placing ourselves there?

Let's re-design our delivery.

PERSONAL DEVELOPMENT EXERCISE

- What is your starting point?
- Where do you want to go?
- Now think like a seagull – and create a new route.

Day 39

Vision

When I take off my glasses
everything becomes unclear.
For there is no clarity.

Everything is a blur
with shade and forms merging
into one another and

as night approaches
streetlights create a
forest of brightness trees.

It is a landscape
without definition.
For there is no clarity.

And yet this lack of definition
creates a totality and a oneness
that is at ease with itself.

Take off your glasses and
you will see more clearly
where there is no clarity.

PERSONAL DEVELOPMENT EXERCISE

- What is your vision? What do you want to see happen in your life?
- Can you step outside of the way that you normally think for a moment? (take your glasses off)
- Without this usual perspective (in this lack of clarity), what do you see? Keep looking.

Day 40

Thinking Outside the Box

Imagine if we go through this time
not asking the real questions.
What if our focus is solely
on present events?

Do we not realise
that there was a time
when we were not here?
An eternity before we existed.

And do we not realise
there will be a time
when we will not be here?
An eternity still to come.

PERSONAL DEVELOPMENT EXERCISE

- Look beyond present events and list the 'real questions' for you.
- How are you planning to find the answers?

Day 41

Instant Loans

Lend your love today
to someone far away
in another country
who is struggling,
with no basic resources,
or help for their family
and who can see no future.

Connect with them now
for just one minute.
Reach out to them
at a personal level
as their father or mother,
as their son or daughter,
in our family of one.

Think of them now.
For this will become
the greatest thing
that you ever do.
Changing everything
in an instant.
Lend your love today.

PERSONAL DEVELOPMENT EXERCISE

- In this one minute you can connect beyond all geography and technology to be with someone who desperately needs help. Sit quietly and be one with them.

Day 42

Rewind

Let us not go back to how it was.
Let us not go back to our old way.
For our future is forwards
not backwards.
Let us not repeat it all again
for we will never be the same again.

New ways of working,
new ways of communicating,
new ways of living,
new ways of thinking,
and a different way of being
are now part of each of us.

When we step out through the door
we can plan a different future.
And then, when we look back
we will see that this was the moment
when we changed.
The moment we changed everything.

PERSONAL DEVELOPMENT EXERCISE

- How have you changed over the last forty-two days?
- What is different about the way you work, communicate, live and the way you think about everything?
- What is your different future?

Day 43

Blockchain

With blocks of information
being passed digitally
from person to person,
we can track every
financial transaction in the chain.
We can always go right back
to the source.
the first block in the chain.

Likewise, every time we reach out
to help someone,
we begin to build a chain
from person to person.
that spreads forever.
We create blockchains of kindness.
We are the source,
the first block in the chain.

PERSONAL DEVELOPMENT EXERCISE

- Think of one person you could help today. As a result of your input, what might they do, or do better?
- Each of us encounters hundreds of blockchain kindness opportunities (BKO) every day. Some are as simple as saying thank you, sending a text or offering some advice. Starting from now, list the next ten BKOs you see today.

Day 44

Response Rate

When I shake the little tree
every single leaf responds.

Instantly, hundreds of leaves
all wave back to me.

They shimmer enthusiastically as one,
each in their own unique way.

PERSONAL DEVELOPMENT EXERCISE

- What tree will you shake today?
- What are you responding to enthusiastically with others as one?

Day 45

Workload

Be thankful for the tasks
you have to do today.
For there will come a time
when those seeking your help
or needing your input,
will no longer be asking.
There will come a time
when you will not be able to help.

PERSONAL DEVELOPMENT EXERCISE

- What are your priority tasks today?
- Can you look beyond the activity to further explore the relationships involved in each task?

Day 46

Road Works

There is a blockage,
a huge boulder in the road
right in front of me.

I've been looking at it for years.
I'm now right up against it
and I must decide what to do.

To continue standing here looking
at the boulder in the road
or to move it.

What's on the other side
of this boulder in the road?
Where does this road lead?

So, this is not a physical challenge
for I would have moved
the boulder in the road years ago.

It's a spiritual challenge.
It's one of becoming and being.
It's my boulder in the road.

PERSONAL DEVELOPMENT EXERCISE

- What is your 'spiritual challenge'?
- How will you move this 'boulder in the road'?
- Where are you on your journey of 'becoming and being'?

Day 47

Harvesting

Every conversation is a story.
Every person we meet is a case study.
Every situation offers options.
Every thought can open a new door.
Every job teaches us new skills.
Every task produces opportunities.
Every memory holds real treasure
for we grow through all things.

Every moment holds an asset for us
enabling us to make sense of life,
helping us with a different perspective
and to find our best way.
So, do not forget your stories.
Please write down your case studies,
explore all of your options and open new doors.
Harvest all that you are today.

PERSONAL DEVELOPMENT EXERCISE

- Begin to build your 'harvest' files and folders on your computer or laptop. Start to collect all your experience, notes, writings, reports, ideas and stories together into relevant folders.
- What will you harvest from yesterday and today?
- Devote some time to harvesting every day. Look at what is emerging for you.

Day 48

The Complete Works

We only have one version of the story.
We can only define what we see as reality
from our perspective.
We view everything
through our personal filters.

Others too have their version of the story.
Each person tries to make sense of life
through their personal filter.
Billions of realities across the world
and all different.

And beyond all of this is
the reality of completeness.
This sees and links everything
and everyone as we truly are.
The complete works.

PERSONAL DEVELOPMENT EXERCISE

- Think of three people you know or work with. In a sentence describe how they each see you.
- Where and how do these views differ from how you picture yourself?

Day 49

Ownership

There is no such thing as mine.
It is there for all of us.
For as soon as we claim
something for ourselves,
we lessen its potential and
we limit our capacity for growth.

Let us shift from ownership and self
to potential and possibilities.
Let us leave all in that sacred space
that we cannot own
so that through sharing and service
we become all that we should be.

PERSONAL DEVELOPMENT EXERCISE

- What do you own?
- What is it that are you be holding onto that in some way may limit you?

Day 50

Behaviour Modification

Deep programming, social conditioning and learned behaviours
cause us to think this way or behave in that way.
We have learned what works for us and what doesn't.
It is easy to see why we continue to confine our thinking
to that which we know or are used to.

Our current levels of understanding and routine behaviour
have hidden other routes and areas of unknowing.
What should we be doing that we haven't even thought of?
We need to find a way through, around,
above or beyond our knowledge base.

Perhaps we need to go deeper than our normal dialogue.
Perhaps we need new conversations, perspectives and insights.
For this time is about making connections
with pieces that we may not know
to deliver a dream that we would never have imagined.

PERSONAL DEVELOPMENT EXERCISE

- What are your areas of unknowing?
- What new connections might you explore that you have never
  even thought of before?
- What is the dream that you have never imagined?

Day 51

Determination

Early this morning as I sat in the woods,
I spotted a young woman jogging in all her gear.
She was pushing her pram and baby
in front of her as she ran,
maintaining a steady pace.
I thought to myself 'what determination!'

About ten minutes later she approached
where I was sitting and reading.
I looked up and said
'I think you're marvellous, absolutely amazing!'
She looked at me, laughed and replied, 'thank you!',
without changing her pace.

Sometimes when we try
to get across the true meaning of a word,
the definition is not enough and
an image can perhaps capture it better.
'Determination' for me will always be
a young woman running with her pram.

PERSONAL DEVELOPMENT EXERCISE

- What does determination mean to you? What's your image?
- How is your determination made real and visible each day?

Day 52

Messenger

When you were born
you were given
a message for the world.

As you live your life
you will uncover and understand
this message.

And then, for the rest of your life
you must share your
message with the world.

PERSONAL DEVELOPMENT EXERCISE

- How much of your message have you uncovered?
- Write down what you understand and what you have yet to make sense of the unanswered questions.
- Your message (however incomplete) is your purpose. Be brave and be true to yourself. How can you share who you really are today?

Day 53

Yield

Give way.
Let others win.
Operate at a higher level.

Give way.
Let it all pass you by.
Stay detached in your own place.

Give way.
Let your rate of return
be what cannot be measured.

PERSONAL DEVELOPMENT EXERCISE

- What are you trying to win?
- Who are you competing with at work or at home?
- How do you measure your yield – your rate of return?

Day 54

Cause and Effect

If you move sideways
you'll get a better view.
If you take a few steps back,
you'll make bigger jumps.

If you need to stop for breath,
you've already gone too far.
If you laugh and smile,
you'll learn to enjoy yourself.

If you feed someone,
you'll not go hungry.
If you stop and plan your route,
you won't go around in circles.

If you are tired,
you can rest.
If you close your eyes,
you'll see more clearly.

If you can sit in silence,
you'll hear the answer.

PERSONAL DEVELOPMENT EXERCISE

- Which of the above nine statements holds the most meaning to you at the moment?
- How will you act on this?

Day 55

Lost

We tend to think of being lost
as a negative thing. It seems to indicate
that we've gone off our path,
gone astray or lost our way
or are not where we should be.

But perhaps the opposite is true.
Perhaps being lost is an opportunity
to find a different way,
be in a different place,
or to explore something new.

I remember on holiday when I was young
my mum sitting with a map on her knee,
my dad always driving 'too fast' and missing
the right turns. He would never go back!
He would always find a new way.

So, can we deliberately choose to be lost?
Can we step out of our predictability
and discover an unfamiliar route?
Can we put ourselves in situations that
lead to a different set of outcomes?

PERSONAL DEVELOPMENT EXERCISE

- In what way has your life become predictable? In what areas are you yearning for something different?

- How might you step out of 'more of the same'? How could you take a different way and get lost?

Day 56

Minimum Wage

As we emerge cautiously into
a different world, what will we
bring to this new normal?

What have we learned
that will now make life better
for us, our family and for others?

How will we relate
to all others without regard
for status, income or position?

For we have learned that those
who were paid nothing or so little
have become our champions.

They have turned our thinking
upside down and empowered us
with compassion to change everything.

So, as we emerge cautiously into
a different world, what will we
bring to this new normal?

PERSONAL DEVELOPMENT EXERCISE

- Kindness and compassion are often excluded in job descriptions. Where do they sit in your role?
- How have you changed over recent weeks? What have you learned?
- What will you bring to the 'new normal'?

Day 57

Leadership

Leadership is not about changing roles
or shifting direction.
It is not about team development
or business strategy.

Leadership is a fundamental shift
in our being—what we are, how we think,
the priorities we set
and how we behave.

Leadership is a behavioural,
emotional and spiritual process.
It's rewiring the hard disk of our being
for a completely different output.

We are no longer
mass market products
of the consumer age
but pilgrims with a purpose.

PERSONAL DEVELOPMENT EXERCISE

- What does it mean to be a 'pilgrim with a purpose'?
- What are your outputs?
- How can you rewire your being for a different type of leadership?

Day 58

Hide and Seek

Come out from under your duvet.
We need to see you.
It's a beautiful sunny morning.
We need to hear from you.

Come out from yourself.
We need you to be with us.
It's your day to shine.
We need you to help us.

PERSONAL DEVELOPMENT EXERCISE

- How have you been hiding recently?
- How will you shine today?

Day 59

Building Services

There are people looking to
build a better world.
They're looking beyond
business models and technology.
They're looking at the development
of a collective approach
with a collaboration of ideas and support
defined by service.

This is a different model and
way outside of the business box.
It is defining what we are about
in a different way.
It is about setting
different expectations of ourselves,
proactively supporting those we know
and those we do not know.

PERSONAL DEVELOPMENT EXERCISE

- What is your model for working with others?
- How are you proactively working with others to build a better world?

Day 60

Resilience

We spend all our lives doing stuff.
Then planning and doing more stuff.
It's exhausting.

Our life is passing us by.
And still we plan
and do more stuff.

Schedules, routines and to do lists.
They strap us into
this world of doing. Like chains.

We accept this as normal
and yet it doesn't have to be like this.
We can get off the treadmill.

Step back from the world of doing
and see a different place.
The world of being.

Here, all is calm and peaceful.
There are no timetables
and no demands.

It's a timeless place
that holds all that is important to us.
Yet many of us rarely go there.

Get off the treadmill every now and then.
You will immediately arrive at the world of being
with its peace, gentleness and with nothing to do.

Just be. Be yourself.
Let all love fill you and renew you
for the next part of your doing journey.

This is the font of resilience.
The origin of all.
This is where we all can be truly ourselves.

It is our place of being where we truly belong.

PERSONAL DEVELOPMENT EXERCISE

- What is the 'stuff' that can trap or exhaust you at times?
- When will you step back and take a little time to refresh yourself at your font of resilience?

Day 61

Disciplinary Hearing

You must never lose
your battle cry or
your willingness to go for it.

You must never dilute
what you once dreamt about,
what you saw so clearly.

You must never give up
no matter what happens,
no matter what others may say.

PERSONAL DEVELOPMENT EXERCISE

- What did you once see so clearly?
- How can you discover (or re-discover) your battle cry?

Day 62

Lifetime Guarantee

We are all made of pure love.
The same pure love is present
in each of us and
unites all of us together.

Our lives add a
rough crust of worldliness
over this pure love,
hiding who and what we truly are.

Life's circumstances, difficulties
and personal choices
can add layer upon layer,
burying our real selves.

But underneath it all,
no matter what we do
exists our pure love,
secure and untarnished.

And so it is, that each of us
and all of us together,
are protected and
cared for, forever.

PERSONAL DEVELOPMENT EXERCISE

- What does your 'rough crust of worldliness' look like?
- What 'life circumstances, difficulties and personal choices' have contributed to hiding your real self?

Day 63

Coffee Morning

I just love this first cup of coffee
in the morning.
It's my moment of appreciation
for the day I've been given.

For it's my celebration and gratitude
for a new start
full of wonder of all that will unfold
before me and for me.

I gently leave to one side
the troubles from yesterday.
I do not carry
the worries of the past.

I begin afresh.
Right here, right now.
With both hands clasped in thanks
around this first cup of coffee.

PERSONAL DEVELOPMENT EXERCISE

- How do you welcome and say thanks for each new day that you have been given? It can be as simple as a thoughtful cup of coffee!
- What does your start to a new day consist of?

Day 64

Self-actualization

Mission and purpose ask us to
reach into ourselves and
try to understand who we are,
why we are here and what
we are meant to do at this time.

Self-actualization is made real
and visible for us every day
through this ongoing inward search
and the ever-present uncovering
of truth on our lifelong journey.

PERSONAL DEVELOPMENT EXERCISE

- What is your mission and purpose?
- What have you uncovered today about yourself?

Day 65

Step Change

Back to work.
Back to the coffee shop.
Back to family and friends.
Back to barbecues.

Back to days out.
Back to meeting up.
Back to school.
Back to all we love.

Progress now means
that we move forwards
by going backwards
in small steps.

We are rediscovering
and cherishing
all that we had and
once took for granted.

PERSONAL DEVELOPMENT EXERCISE

- What is the 'step change' you are most looking forward to rediscovering?
- How do you express your thanks and appreciation for what you already have in all aspects of your life?

Day 66

Hands On

I can remember you
washing your hands in the kitchen sink.
You'd just come home from work
with garage grease up to your elbows.
And Ma rescued the situation with a towel
whilst serving us our tea.

I can remember you
asking me to hold out my hands
so that you could wind the wool into balls.
And you'd sit at night
knitting Aran jumpers
that were admired by all.

PERSONAL DEVELOPMENT EXERCISE

- Being hands-on means that we are actively involved. We make things happen with others. What are you making happen at the moment?
- What hands-on activities do you have with your partner and/or children in the daily activities of home life?
- How are you working with others who are holding out their hands, asking for help?

Day 67

Exclusion

It is no longer enough
to stand inside
the tent and
call people to join you.

Sometimes we need to go
outside the tent and
work with people
so that we can all walk in together.

PERSONAL DEVELOPMENT EXERCISE

- Who is in your tent?
- How can I or others join you?

Day 68

Net Gain

If you pull back the net curtain
you will see clearly.
You will see forever
into the distance.

If you don't pull back the net curtain
all you will see is
the net curtain and
a vague light behind it.

PERSONAL DEVELOPMENT EXERCISE

- What would you like to see more clearly?
- What is the net curtain?

Day 69

Connections

I know that I am nothing
but that I am connected
to everything through love.

I know that I can do so little
but through this great love
I can do everything.

I therefore give myself to love
so that everyone can be well and
all as it should be.

In submitting to infinite goodness
I unleash a gentle power within me
beyond all imagining.

For it is in this complete submission
that I am connected to everything
that ever was and is yet to come.

PERSONAL DEVELOPMENT EXERCISE

- What are you connected to?
- Who are you connected to?

Day 70

Honours List

I worry about what has happened,
forgetting all is a privilege.
I regret the mess I've made
forgetting all is a privilege.
I feel disappointed by what I've done
forgetting all is a privilege.

Each day brings an ongoing torrent
of privileges, opportunities and gifts.
Irrespective of how well I manage these,
the torrent continues.
And so, as I try to embrace what happens today
I remember that all is a privilege.

PERSONAL DEVELOPMENT EXERCISE

- What privileges, opportunities and gifts have you already received today?
- How will you embrace and use these?

Day 71

Priorities

I've run out of time.
I tick the boxes
get halfway through
but the end of the list
never gets done.
I just don't have the time.

I start afresh each day.
I re-write my list and
put my priorities at the top.
But the important tasks
never get done.
I run out of time.

It's the same routine
as I set out the tasks.
And then it hits me
that the real stuff never
even gets onto my list.
Never gets done.

PERSONAL DEVELOPMENT EXERCISE

- What is the real stuff for you?
- How will you rethink and reorganise your day to get the real stuff done?

Day 72

Trial and Error

My failures remind me
that I am still on the right path.
They point me again
in the right direction.
They encourage me
as I start again.

This is not about
determination or effort.
Rather it is about
the gift of grace
which opens the window
to let the light in.

PERSONAL DEVELOPMENT EXERCISE

- What are your failures?
- How would you describe the gift of grace that enables you to start again?

Day 73

Climate Change

Throw open the windows.
Kick open the doors.
Let the sunshine in.

It's been dull and dreary here for too long.
It's sapped your energy
and killed your enthusiasm.

Escape from the prison
of expectation, routine
and just getting by.

All is there before you.
Waiting expectantly.
And now you are free.

Go to new places
Meet everyone who needs you and
work with them to make a difference.

Explode now with warmth.
Do everything you should.
Do all that you can.

PERSONAL DEVELOPMENT EXERCISE

- How will you escape from the prison of expectation, routine and just getting by?
- What will you do with this new freedom?

Day 74

Investment Strategy

When we speak of investment
we think of the financial return on our money.
But this is not investment,
this is just making more money – or trying to.

If we really want a return on our resources
then we should invest in the skills, experience
knowledge and passions of all the people
we know and those we don't know.

And we don't do this for financial gain.
We do it because we have money
and because we can help them
to become what they should be.

This is e real investment
helping people to be all they can be
and in turn enabling us to be
who we should be.

When we die we will have no money.
We can't take it with us.
So, plan to invest all you can whilst you can
and watch the fruits grow whilst you're still here.

Create ripples of goodness.
Plant seeds of hope.
Invest in all that is positive and kind.
Make your mark on all those you meet.

Invest your time helping others.
Go way beyond duty or expectation.
Surprise others with your commitment,
your energy, your enthusiasm and your spirit.

PERSONAL DEVELOPMENT EXERCISE

- Who is your investment strategy focussed on?
- What is the return on your resources?

Day 75

Semi-detached

It's obvious to all of us
how the tasks, worries and
responsibilities of daily life
can wear us down.

We also know from experience
that these all pass in due course,
but still we get overcome at times
with the demands upon us.

It is in the quieter moments
when life is less hectic
that we appreciate the peace and
gentleness that lies beneath everything.

This is where we really belong.
And so, our daily focus must be
to stay semi-detached and balance
being busy in our world yet quiet in ourselves.

PERSONAL DEVELOPMENT EXERCISE

- What are the tasks and worries of daily life that can wear you down?
- When and where do you have your quieter moments?
- Can you make time each day to stay semi-detached?

Day 76

Reminders

Never too old,
never too tired,
never too late,
never too much trouble.

Always enough,
always great,
always yes,
always love.

PERSONAL DEVELOPMENT EXERCISE

- Write another two phrases beginning with 'never ...'
- Write another two phrases beginning with 'always ...'

Day 77

Inclusion Manager

God has a different relationship
with every single person.
He communicates with us and
works with each of us in different ways.

We all have different roles and each
role is equal, vital, personal and unique.
The unbeliever and the monk.
We all share the same space.

PERSONAL DEVELOPMENT EXERCISE

- If 'Inclusion Manager' is another name for God, how is your role
  equal, vital, personal and unique?
- What is this 'same space' that we all share?

Day 78

Multi-tasking

Our task is to continually
seek the truth,
not just to listen to others
or be influenced by popular opinion.

Our task is to listen
to what is deep within us,
not to follow the crowd
or miss the real conversations.

Our task is to live
the life given to us,
in full without reservation, without excuses
without blinkers each day.

Our task is to become
all that we should be,
to be our own person, there for others,
the helper and peace builder.

Our task is to uncover
and use our gifts and skills to help others,
not to build wealth
or to become important.

Our task is to set
our own course and not be buffeted
by events and activities around us,
or what pleases others.

Our task is to reach out
to all others, especially those who are hungry
and those who ask for our help,
in any way today.

Our task is to love,
to be a source of encouragement and a guide,
so that we all may become
what we can be.

PERSONAL DEVELOPMENT EXERCISE

- Go through each of the eight tasks above and make a note for your to-do list this week.
- Which of the above tasks holds most potential for you?

Day 79

Time and Motion

Grasp every moment.
Waste not one second.
Fill each minute with joy
and gratitude.

Seize opportunities.
Show your enthusiasm.
Excite others.
Pass on your love.

Surprise people.
Make them smile.
Waste not one second.
Grasp every moment.

PERSONAL DEVELOPMENT EXERCISE

- Time and motion studies help us to evaluate how effective we are. A typical day contains over 50,000 seconds. How did you do yesterday?
- Did you seize opportunities, show your enthusiasm, excite others, pass on your love, surprise people and make them smile?

Day 80

Mentor

I'm not vey good at the meditation thing,
so for me, it's a morning business meeting with God.
We chat through priorities and tasks.

We look at the current focus
in line with the overall strategy
and identify people we need to talk to.

We come up with a few good ideas together
and set out a detailed plan for the day.
We all need a mentor.

PERSONAL DEVELOPMENT EXERCISE

- Who is your mentor?
- Who do you mentor?

Day 81

Peace Talks

She gently reminds me that
any fool can fall out with someone.
But I feel really angry,
betrayed and let down.
She explains that the reality is that
we are still connected
no matter what happens.

It may seem like the end
of the road, but before
your angry outburst,
that long legal case begins
or that explosive email is sent
just remember that this is not
the end of your story together.

For you will connect again
sooner than you think.
So, always part on good terms.
Think well of the other
no matter what,
for both of you are forever
part of each other's journey.

Let the anger go and be at peace
with yourself and others.
Speak well of those who let you down,
for in time they will have
no answer to your kindness
but kindness itself.
Any fool can fall out.

PERSONAL DEVELOPMENT EXERCISE

- Who is it that you do not always 'think well of' or 'speak well of'?
- If you were your own life coach how would you help yourself to let go of this anger?

Day 82

Interior Design

I'm using this time
as an opportunity to rethink where I am
and to start afresh.

I even moved
all my office furniture around yesterday
and it made a huge difference.

You see, I'm now able to
look out of the window at the trees
and not stare at the wall.

Moving the furniture around
has literally changed how I see things.
It's my interior design process.

PERSONAL DEVELOPMENT EXERCISE

- How could you rearrange your furniture for a different perspective?
- How could you rearrange your day for a different set of outcomes?

Day 83

Scenario Planning

There are many ways.
You have your own way.
And your way has
many options and possibilities.

Stay on your own path.
It may be muddled or uncertain now
but it will become clear.
Be yourself.

Stay true to yourself
and to all those who love (and have loved) you
for they too are on the path
of love and uncertainty.

Love all others
for your kindness (with a smile and a helping hand)
can be a signpost on their journey.
And yours.

You have a fixed amount of time
So use every moment to work for love.
All else will pass.
Love is.

PERSONAL DEVELOPMENT EXERCISE

- What are your options and possibilities?
- How would you describe 'your way"?

Day 84

Merchandising

Rearrange yourself.
Mix up your pieces a bit
and bring out
all the love you have.
Re-stock your shelves.
Let the world see
a new you, the real you.

PERSONAL DEVELOPMENT EXERCISE

- What can I get in your shop?
- What is your new merchandising plan?

Day 85

Retail Training Program

Go to a bookstore and browse.
Check out the poetry, personal development
or business books.

Collect stories, ideas, quotes and perspectives
that challenge or excite you.
Let your sense of wonder come alive.

Let possibilities and scenarios
explode in your brain like winter fireworks.
Capture the key messages.

Next time you go shopping, join me
and let us take ten minutes together
on our retail training program.

PERSONAL DEVELOPMENT EXERCISE

- Pick out two or three books from your shelf or bookcase that you haven't opened for ages. Browse through and write down three or four ideas. Now play with these and think 'How can I use these ideas?'

- Join me next time you go shopping on my Retail Training Program.

Day 86

Annual Performance Review

Your time is running out.
Another year has gone.
Your life is passing by.

It is here now.
The moment to grasp
all that is meant to be.

The whole purpose
and meaning
of your life.

Your time is running out.
Another year has gone.
Your life is passing by.

It is here now.
The moment to grasp
all that is meant to be.

PERSONAL DEVELOPMENT EXERCISE

- This is the key moment in your life. What will you grasp?
- What will you achieve by this time next year – at your next annual performance review?

Day 87

Tea Bags

When you sit and look
into your cup of tea
what do you see
when it is finished?

Years ago, fortune tellers
would predict our future
by looking at the pattern of the leaves
resting at the bottom of the cup.

Tea bags now mean that we
throw away our tea leaves
before we drink our tea,
leaving no clues, no predictions.

So, as you gently dispose
of your tea bag today,
take a moment to imagine your future
and how your story will unfold.

PERSONAL DEVELOPMENT EXERCISE

- Can you imagine how your life might unfold in terms of work, relationships and all that is important to you?
- What is the one surprise or unexpected event?
- Write out the perfect story for your future.

Day 88

Three Hundred and Sixty Degree Feedback

Love is not something we have to search for.
Love is with us, beside us,
and in us always
no matter what.

So, this journey of life is an inward one,
to be love in all we are
and an outward one,
to love all who we meet.

PERSONAL DEVELOPMENT EXERCISE

- What does your love look like – inside and out?
- List and celebrate the top five real, practical and visible outputs of your love.

Day 89

Business Drivers

Are you the driver?
This is the question I was asked
when paying for tea and a scone in the cafe
by the ancient monastic site at Clonmacnoise, in Ireland.

I guess it was my solitary nature, the sunglasses or
absence of a camera that led to her question.
I was clearly not part of the Japanese tourist group.
Now, every day, I ask myself: 'Are you the driver?'

PERSONAL DEVELOPMENT EXERCISE

- What are the drivers in your business or work?
- What are you driving?

Day 90

Happy Father's Day

Every time I play golf
I am with you, remembering
to keep my head down
and watch the ball.

I always want to play
on my own, partly due to
embarrassment at my standard
but also, just to be with you.

For it is not about the score,
the lost balls, my swing, or even
the one or two good shots
that redeem the round.

It's about being with you,
treasuring the gift that you gave me,
and remembering your call
to follow through.

PERSONAL DEVELOPMENT EXERCISE

- What are your best memories of those who loved you?
- What is your 'follow through'?

Day 91

Relocation Package

We're moving house next week. My wife is busy ensuring all the lightbulbs are working. She will clean the flat from top to bottom. She's had new window locks fitted as we'd lost the keys.

We've been to the hardware store and bought a new electric fire to replace the one that we are taking. The Shop Assistant laughed as it was the hottest summer on record! We have even bought better quality ornamental coals for the gas fire.

We've touched up all the paperwork where pictures used to hang. We have left a welcome pack of notes with instructions on the boiler, door key codes, internet connections, recycling arrangements and heating controls. The last thing will be to leave a bunch of flowers and a bottle of wine.

We've spent all this time and we will never see the people who move in. We will not know who takes our place here. We will not know if they are kind or thoughtful. We will not know if they are younger or older than us.

When I questioned all this activity, I am gently reminded that it's just about doing for others as we would like them to do for us. She asks 'If we were to walk in here what would we like to see?

It's not so much about us leaving and moving but, them arriving. Sometimes we need to relocate our thinking. For relocation is not so much about where you go but what you leave behind.

(P.S. Three weeks after we left, we received a lovely thank-you card)

PERSONAL DEVELOPMENT EXERCISE

- What is your next move in life or work?
- What will you leave behind?

Day 92

Peace Building

Throw your grenades
of love into the world
with a quiet thought.

Fire your missiles
of help to those in need
with a wish especially for them.

Blast your kindness
to everyone you have never met
with a moment of silence for them.

Launch your propaganda offensive
with words and messages of love
and a share of your resources.

Create collateral damage
that inspires and transforms everyone
to join your war of peace.

PERSONAL DEVELOPMENT EXERCISE

- What is your war of peace?
- How can you escalate this?

Day 93

Compliance

To change things for the better
You do not need to operate within
the rules of business
and the machinery of the world.
You can bypass the games of competition
and expectations of others.

You have your own compass of compliance,
your own way of being
and are your own self.
This must grow and flourish
despite all around it and
because of all around it.

You can set a different path.
A new way.
You can offer fresh hope
just by being totally and truthfully you.
This will create new ways of working
that will change everything – forever.

PERSONAL DEVELOPMENT EXERCISE

- What guides your compass of compliance?
- How are you changing things for the better?

Day 94

Territory Management

God is not territorial. God is love.
God does not need us to believe in anything but love.
For love is all we need to unite us in common goals
of peace, kindness and compassion.

Love requires us to look beyond ourselves.
It asks us to feed the hungry and care for the sick.
Questions of belief or non-belief miss the point
of all that is.

We are not here to exclude others
but to unite ourselves with all others.
That is our purpose.
There is no greater priority for mankind.

Structures give authority
and authority brings power over others.
Religious structures too can divide us
despite all the good words.

We can walk through the doors of exclusion
and re-write the rules that hinder
the fulfilment of the true purpose,
potential and happiness of all.

Inclusion can grow quietly and
gently within each of us,
for this is our personal journey
of love.

PERSONAL DEVELOPMENT EXERCISE

- What exclusive structures do we belong to or support?
- Who are we not linking up with or reaching out to, that we should?

Day 95

Reset Button

If we keep thinking
the same way
we will come to the same conclusion.

If we keep doing
the same things
we will still get the same results.

If we keep looking
the same way
we will miss what is really happening.

If we keep going in
the same direction
we will miss the turning point.

Press your reset button.
Think differently
about everything.

PERSONAL DEVELOPMENT EXERCISE

- What will happen when you press your reset button?
- How will you think differently, do things differently, see things differently and go in a different way?

Day 96

World Wide Web

The World Wide Web has existed
since the beginning of time.
It has enabled people to link up and
help one another without limitation.

If we say a prayer today
for someone in need who we don't know
we can reach out with love
and we will change the world.

For our gift of love will explode
like a million meteor showers,
exploding together at once
and covering the whole world.

These explosions of love
will in turn create more explosions of love.
In an instant we can change,
help and support the lives of everyone.

The exponential growth of love,
beyond culture, countries or technology
is personal, direct and transformative.
It's our World Wide Web of love.

PERSONAL DEVELOPMENT EXERCISE

- Send out a message on the World Wide Web of love.
- Where will your meteor showers land?

Day 97

Jigsaw Puzzle

I do not even have one piece of the jigsaw.
I don't know how many pieces there are
or what the picture on the lid of the box is.

Yet this is a jigsaw that will be completed.
For the search for pieces and the piecing together
will answer every question.

PERSONAL DEVELOPMENT EXERCISE

- What pieces have you found so far?
- What pieces are missing?

Day 98

Angels

Isabella is the light of my life,
saving me from everything.
Not expecting anything
and finding true joy in all things.

She helps me with mundane tasks
bringing me to a level of understanding,
peace and real happiness
in these moments.

Her excited greeting 'Hello Grandad!'
makes me thankful for my years.
Her run to get lifted
makes me wish I was younger.

Isabella is my angel.

PERSONAL DEVELOPMENT EXERCISE

- Who is your angel?
- How does your angel save you?

Day 99

Time Zone

I've changed my time zone.
I now get up at six o'clock rather than eight
and go to bed at ten o'clock rather than midnight.

By moving my time zone back two hours
I have not only been able to redesign my day
but to reinvent the work that I do.

You see, these two amazing extra hours
every morning help me to redefine
not just the rest of the day but who I am.

PERSONAL DEVELOPMENT EXERCISE

- How could you restructure your daily routine in some way to create 'extra' time?
- How would you like to reinvent the work that you do?

Day 100

Uniqueness

These writings reflect me and my journey. They're published in order to encourage you to capture and explore every moment, opportunity and wonderful event of your journey.

Go where your heart takes you. Have moments and days of different thoughts and experiences. Get off the worldly commute and see the countryside. Go without your satnav.

Every moment can hold something amazing for it is a doorway to understanding. Do not settle for more or better but for understanding, insight, perspective and personal truth.

Create your own crazy life journey. Make it up as you go along. Enjoy every minute especially failures, disappointments, illness and fatigue for these are the reminders of who we truly are.

Share your successes with humility and use these to encourage others. Fire them up with joy and enthusiasm. Hold out your hand and offer to help. Surprise others with a call. For the more you reach out, the more you learn about yourself.

We build our own truth from the building blocks we have been given, such as our DNA, our health, our parents, our culture, our schooling, our religious upbringing, our gifts and talents and much more.

So, it is no surprise that many of the concepts, ideas and sayings that we pick up early in life are reflected in who we become. 'Go with the flow' is what my Dad said. 'If it's worth doing it's worth doing right.' was another.

These messages from our foundation years are always with us. But they are only seeds for us to water. They are the raw material for us to grow, shape, form, build, develop and to create something unique.

This is the key purpose of our lives, to be a unique structure, a unique creation and a unique offering of love in the world. It doesn't matter how we do this, for each journey is of its own.

We do not have to follow the traditions of the past, the beliefs of the present or the technology terms and conditions of the future. All these can trap and enslave us.

Our task is to learn and enjoy being fully ourselves in this life. For life is meant to be a process of joy. If we can understand this we will see beyond the difficulties, suffering, pain and death that we must endure. This is the quest.

No one perspective, teaching, or personal development book will get you there. Life is an ongoing personal development process. Only you can know what is going on within you and what makes real sense. There is, in my experience, no quick fix or instant download.

Our worldly attachment to power, position, money, instant satisfaction, ego, vanity and self-centredness all work against this complete understanding of who we are. And yet, these are so often part of the daily reality of our lives.

But there can and there will be, moments of light, glimpses of understanding and instances where we see things differently. These are the stepping-stones for uncovering our path.

Every life with its glamour or failures, with its successes or poverty holds its own unique, beautiful and infinitely precious journey of understanding. This is the wonder of life for we are born with nothing and we die with nothing. The only thing in between is our journey of understanding.

Help everyone to have the courage to step outside of the norm, to take time for themselves, to be different, to listen and to offer us ideas and perspectives that most of this world would find strange, crazy or unrealistic. Let us all be an inspiration of difference and acceptance. Let us all go with the flow and see where it takes us.

The beliefs of another are no threat to you. The traditions and practices of your neighbour should be the greatest joy especially if you disagree with them or 'just don't get it'. For we all should celebrate not just our uniqueness but our ability to be different in a world that drives conformity, control and standardisation.

We need creativity, innovation, compassion and we need new perspectives. We need different ways of dealing with the new challenges the world is facing. Let us all be champions of uniqueness. Encourage others to 'have a go', say what they really think, question values and create better ways of living.

In our interactions with others let this light of uniqueness shine through. A smile, a 'thank you' and encouragement must be part of every conversation. Reaching out to those in need, those who are lonely and those with no one to talk with is our mission of uniqueness.

Our mother and father gave us our DNA and the foundation of our uniqueness for us to grow and become all that we can be. We do the same for our children who then in return do the same for their children.

We are all protected under an umbrella of uniqueness which cannot be troubled, overthrown or destroyed. It is not confined to this world but is there forever, cherishing each of us, as together we build an eternity of love.

PERSONAL DEVELOPMENT EXERCISE

- In what ways are you unique?
- Describe your outlook or philosophy on life.
- What are the key messages you will pass onto your children?
- How can your uniqueness help to build an eternity of love?

Evaluation and Review

Now that you have completed the process it is important to review your learning and outcomes.

1. Evaluate this process

- What were your favourite perspectives?

- Why did you like these?

- When you wrote notes, what did you write about?

- What do you like about this personal development approach of using perspectives for thinking differently about common words?

2. Review your development

- What were the main learning points for you?

- Did you write any perspectives?

- What have you learned about yourself from this process?

- What will be your key action points moving forward?

- What will you do differently from now on?

- When you look back in 12 months' time, what will be the one key thing that you will have achieved or will be different?

3. Use your notes

Look through your journal and highlight the key notes and comments that you have made. Capture these in a summary page (or short document/e-book) – one that you can refer to as you move forward. Use this to encourage and motivate yourself. Keep the priority points on your phone for handy reference.

4. Write your book

Why not create and build your book of perspectives? Write new perspectives for the words I have used in this book and/ or use your own words. Add a new perspective every day.

5. Continue the process

Continue to reflect upon, use and indeed adapt the material in this book. It's meant to be a launchpad for your future.

I hope that you will build upon this process by using the perspectives in one of the other five ways that we outlined at the beginning.

Think about applying the perspectives approach to focus on different areas of your life – such as your work, relationships, spirituality, career development and your future.

6. Beyond the first 100 days

This book covers the first 100 days of my 'Thinking Differently About Everything' blog. You can continue to explore and work with me as I add further perspectives - www.workitout. info/desblog

Pop over any day!

The Workshop

Would your team or organisation benefit from fresh perspectives? Des McCabe delivers the three-hour 'Thinking Differently About Everything' workshop and brings this new learning approach to a wide range of workplaces. The workshop is available on-line or in person for groups of 6-100 people.

For further details please www.workitout.info or contact Des personally at diversiton@gmail.com / 44 7717 203325

Opportunities are available globally for licensed trainers to deliver this workshop, either in-house or as independent consultants/facilitators. Please contact Des for an information pack.

More training and support

Career and work – What do you really want to do?

- See the range of free training materials and resources at www.workitout.info

- Check out Des McCabe's best-selling book - 'Work it Out! – how to find the work you always wanted in a shifting jobs market' (Hay House)

- License Your Training Course – how to offer your courses and services worldwide. Go to www.workitout.info

Email Des McCabe diversiton@gmail.com or call him directly on - 44 7717 203325

Diversity and Inclusion

- Order the Inclusion Calendar at www.diversiton.com for your Organization

- Host the Award-winning Religion and Belief Workshop in your organization. A three hour online or in person workshop. www.diversiton.com

- Apply for the Inclusion Award and the Diversity Champion Award at www.diversitychampion.org

Email Sharon Cowan sharon@diversiton.com or call her directly on - 44 28 417 54777

About the Author

Des McCabe is one of the UK's leading specialists in inclusion and personal development. He is also a best-selling 'Hay House' author.

Des founded and built the largest independent training organisation in the UK, finding work for 5,000 long-term unemployed and helping 4,000 people to get qualifications every year. His expertise in the field of job creation led to him becoming an advisor to the British, Irish, US, Argentinian, Romanian and Albanian governments on employment, social inclusion and training-related policy. He is recognised as one of Europe's leading job creation entrepreneurs by 'Europe's Top 500'.

Beyond his professional achievements, Des established and raised funding for The Training Trust, an international charity set up to meet the humanitarian needs of children in Romanian orphanages, working in partnership with the Romanian Government.

In Africa, Des has been involved in Comic Relief projects in Kenya and has supported a range of anti-poverty work in Ghana and Madagascar. Back in the UK, Des served as Chair of the European Union's cross-border Interreg training group in Northern Ireland, and as Chair of the EU Border Training Bureau. He was an advisor to the Irish and US Governments in the early stages of the Northern Ireland Peace Process and went on to design the 'Peace Builder' training programme with US Special Envoy Senator George Mitchell's Northern Ireland Fund for Reconciliation.

Des received the Diversity 21 Award for the development of an innovative diversity programme on religion and belief. He established Diversiton as a social enterprise and went on to create the leading Diversity and Inclusion Calendars. He works with people across the world on the licensing of their training courses and services.

In 2011 Hay House published Des McCabe's ground-breaking book Work It Out!: How to Find the Work You Always Wanted in a Shifting Jobs Market

Work it Out! programmes (for all ages) are delivered internationally in partnership with Governments and Agencies to support career development, income generation and sustainability, enterprise development, inclusion and integration, rural development, rehabilitation and much more.

The Last Word

The last word for now must go to you! If you have enjoyed this personal development approach to 'Thinking Differently About Everything' please leave a review at Amazon. Just a line or two would great! It is easy to do – go to the book page and click on 'Review this Product' and leave a few words! You might want to give your overall impression or highlight a perspective that you like. Thanks so much!

I'd love to hear your thoughts on this book or any fresh Perspectives that you would like to share. Keep in touch.

Take care,
Des

Contact Details

You can get in touch with Des here:
Email – diversiton@gmail.com
Phone – 44 7717 203325

You can continue your 'Thinking Differently About Everything' journey every day and read the latest perspectives at www.workitout.info/desblog

Linkedn - www.linkedin.com/in/desmccabe
Facebook - DesMcCabeTRAINING
Instagram – @des_mccabe

Index of Perspectives

M

N

O

P

R

Printed in Poland
by Amazon Fulfillment
Poland Sp. z o.o., Wrocław

61407549R00089